FROGS SING SONGS

Written by Yvonne Winer

Illustrated by Tony Oliver

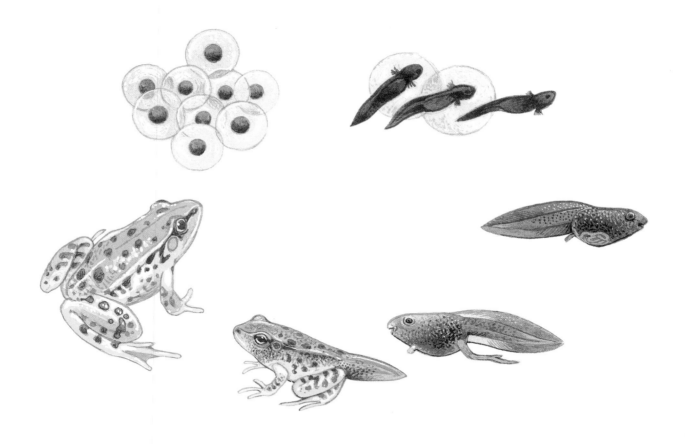

ini Charlesbridge

Frogs sing their songs
From the lakes to the trees.
Rattles and croaks
Create sweet melodies.
That's how frogs sing songs.

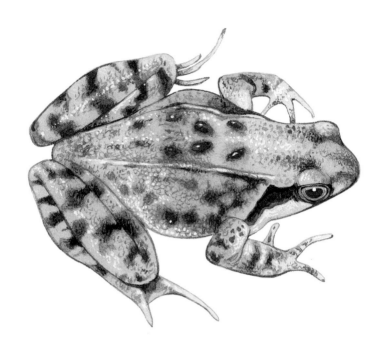

Frogs sing their songs
From a pouch in their throats.
A drumming crescendo
Fills the forest with notes.
That's how frogs sing songs.

Frogs sing their songs
In warm summer rain.
Softly and slowly,
A gentle refrain.
That's how frogs sing songs.

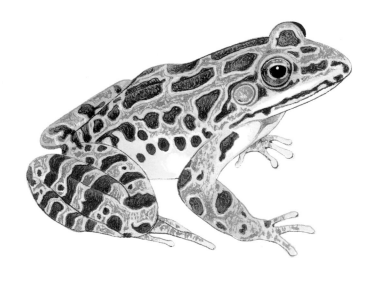

Frogs sing their songs
Discordant and low,
Harsh rolling calls
Where whispering streams flow.
That's how frogs sing songs.

Frogs sing their songs
When day is no more,
Hidden by leaves
On the dark forest floor.
That's when frogs sing songs.

Frogs sing their songs
As night shadows fall.
Mellow the echo
Of their low grunting call.
That's when frogs sing songs.

Frogs sing their songs,
A choral delight.
A low serenade
To herald the night.
That's when frogs sing songs.

Frogs sing their songs,
Their concerts begin,
Echoing far
As mist settles in.
That's when frogs sing songs.

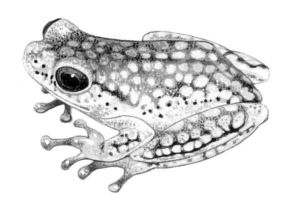

Frogs sing their songs
To an African beat,
By reedy lagoons
In the warm summer heat.
That's where frogs sing songs.

Frogs sing their songs
Where Arctic winds blow,
Sheltering in logs
Beneath blankets of snow.
That's where frogs sing songs.

Frogs sing their songs,
Joyous the sounds.
A trilling ensemble
From rock walls resounds.
That's where frogs sing songs.

Frogs sing their songs,
A cantata for spring—
To welcome the flowers,
And the insects they bring.
That's why frogs sing songs.

Frogs sing their songs,
And they glide through the air.
Graceful their movement,
To a mate waiting there.
That's why frogs sing songs.

Frogs sing their songs,
But polluted dark streams
Threaten their future
And our wilderness dreams.
That's why frogs sing songs.

Frog Identification Guide

Frogs sing songs mainly to find a mate in the spring. They have been around for some 190 million years. Amazingly adaptable, frogs live in habitats ranging from freezing Arctic snow to burning deserts. As they are cold-blooded, their blood temperature is largely dependent on that of the surrounding air.

Frogs can change color to harmonize with their surroundings by the expansion and contraction of pigment cells in their skin. They breathe through lungs, but when inactive, or when temperatures are low, they can breathe through their skin.

Although frogs eat mostly small insects and spiders, they have been known to eat other small creatures. They catch food with their tongue, which is attached to the front of their mouth and is coated with a sticky substance.

Deforestation, acid rain, pollution, over-cultivation, global warming, and the use of agricultural chemicals have all threatened frog habitats, resulting in the destruction of some species. This book celebrates the joy of frog sounds in the hope that they will not be silenced.

Frogs in this guide are arranged in the same order as the pages of this book, but conclude with the frog which appears on the front cover. The small drawing in the left margin is a reduction of the drawing above each poem.

Red-Eyed Tree Frog

Agalychnis callidryas

Central America

This spectacular frog is clad in rich, exotic colors, with blood-red eyes, neon-green back, blue-striped flanks, cream-colored underside and orange-red toepads. Its call sounds like a baby rattle. It inhabits the lowlands and eastern slopes from central Mexico southward to the Panama Canal. It lives in rainforests in trees as high as fifty feet and it descends at dusk to feed.

European Common Frog

Rana temporaria

Europe

This frog inhabits woodlands close to streams, lagoons, and marshes. It emerges at night to hunt small invertebrates. It spends the winter deeply embedded in the soil or under mud in marshes. In spring it enters the water to breed and lay between one and two thousand eggs. Its song is a deep croaking.

Poison Arrow Frog

Dendrobates azureus

South America

This small frog's bright colors warn predators and may help mates defend their territories during courtship. It lives in the jungles and savannahs of Surinam. While the male produces only a very subdued croaking to attract a mate, the female actively courts the male by nudging him and stroking his back.

Pickerel Frog

Rana palustris

North America

This frog is common along the Atlantic seaboard and in the Upper Midwest and ranges from Canada southward to the Carolinas and westward to Minnesota and Texas. It is named after the large pickerel and wall-eyed pike that feed on it. It has few predators, as its skin secretes a toxin. The call of the male is a harsh snore or rolling croak, which sounds a little like tearing cloth.

Asian Horned Frog

Megophrys montana

Southern, eastern, and southeastern Asia

Horned frogs are particularly interesting for the long skin projection on the top of the snout and the triangular pointed appendages similar to horns on each upper eyelid. It is common in virgin forests where it lives in the foliage. It is nocturnal and spends the day hidden under dry leaves on the forest floor. It is a skillful and voracious predator, feeding on various invertebrates.

Northern Leopard Frog

Rana pipiens

North America

These very common frogs eat a varied diet, including leeches, snails, spiders, and many kinds of insects. They also take larger prey such as small fish, tadpoles, smaller frogs, and small snakes. They have even been known to catch small birds. They are very good jumpers and can leap up to fifteen times their body length. Their main song is a low, long, grunting note, followed by several short notes.

White-Lipped Tree Frog

Litoria infrafrenata

Australia and New Guinea

This is the largest tree frog in the world. The female can measure over five inches in body length. Although its color can range from green to brown or sometimes a brownish pink, one feature is constant: a broad white line running along the lower lip. The males descend to the ground to breed. The call consists of two deep notes repeated at short intervals, sounding like the barking of a large dog.

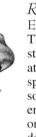

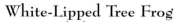

American Bullfrog
Rana catesbeiana

Native to S E Canada, America. Introduced to Hawaii, Mexico, Jamaica, Italy and Japan. The bullfrog is usually found around lakes. It is active both by day and night, and its eating habits are legendary. With its large mouth it will snatch up insects, fish, crayfish, turtles, other frogs, birds, and even small ducks. At dusk and during summer nights the familiar 'jug-o-rum' call of the male can be heard from a great distance. The female can lay over twenty thousand eggs which form a large, wide, floating mass.

Painted Reed Frog
Hyperolius marmoratus
South Africa

There are over two hundred species of reed frogs. Their beautiful patterns and colors can change in response to temperature or background. They are only an inch long. They often live far from water, so escape danger by long bounding leaps. During the dry season they disappear into cracks and crevices in the ground. They emit a shrill, high-pitched whistle.

Wood Frog
Rana sylvatica
North America, Canada, Alaska

Wood frogs can survive the effects of sub-zero temperatures beneath logs, rocks or leaf litter, with up to sixty-five percent of their body water frozen. They manage this by making 'anti-freeze' compounds. Ice on the frog's skin triggers a response that activates glycogen breakdown in the liver, flooding glucose into the blood. As they are found as far north as the Arctic Circle, these frogs are America's northernmost species. Their call sounds like a hoarse quack.

Blue Mountains Tree Frog
Litoria citropa
Australia

This nocturnal tree frog is found throughout eastern Victoria and New South Wales. It is most likely to be seen sitting on rocks, but is sometimes encountered in densely vegetated habitats alongside creeks. The distinctive red and yellow-green splashes of color on this predominantly light-brown frog act as a defense, flashing warning signals to predators, such as snakes, whenever the frog jumps. It measures up to two and a half inches and eats insects. Its call is a harsh scream followed by a trill.

Northern Dwarf Tree Frog
Litoria bicolor
Australia and New Guinea

This small slender species often occurs in huge numbers at the edge of pools and swamps. It is found along the coast and adjacent areas of northern Australia from the Kimberley region to Proserpine in the east. It is also found in the southern coastal areas of New Guinea. Its call is a high-pitched creak followed by several "pips."

Borneo Flying Frog
Rhacophorus pardalis
Borneo

Borneo's flying frogs become airborne from tree to tree or to descend to breeding sites. Loose flaps of skin on their limbs, as well as long webbed fingers and toes, give them the lift they need to glide. Adhesive pads enable tricky landings on tree trunks. Thanks to the extensive webbing, these frogs not only glide, but can make banked turns of 180 degrees in mid-air. Their call is a quiet combination of clicks, rattles, and gurgles.

Asiatic Painted Frog
Kaloula pulchra
Southern China, Borneo, Sulawesi,
South India, Sri Lanka

Although it measures only two to three inches in length, this frog's loud ox-like bellow suggests a much larger animal. It also explains its assortment of nicknames including the Indian Bullfrog and the Ox Frog. It is found in a wide variety of habitats and is very common in parks and gardens. The males emerge from their burrows after heavy rainstorms and congregate in the puddles, sounding off at night to attract mates.

Green and Golden Bell Frog
Litoria aurea
Southeastern Australia

This is a relatively large frog that can measure up to three inches long. It has varying amounts of green and coppery gold on its back. It emits a long, low growl. It is a native of southeastern Australia, mainly along the coast from Byron Bay in New South Wales to Lakes Entrance in Victoria, and also throughout the southern tablelands. Although a member of the tree frog family, it spends most of its time in the water, on the ground, or on low reeds and does not usually climb trees. Once one of the most commonly encountered frogs, it has now disappeared completely from over ninety percent of its former range and is considered endangered.

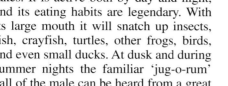
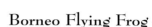

Author's dedication

In memory of my parents Edwin and Nettie Jay and my brother Vic.
Also to my other siblings and their families who shared the frog song
of our beautiful farm 'Ripplemead' on the South African Highveld:
Ted and Norma Jay, Max and Lil Joubert, and Jean and DeVille Roos.

Acknowledgments

To Jennifer Woodman who provided so much
editorial assistance in the early drafts of all my books.
For friendship and support.

References

Amphibian Species of the World ed. by Darrel R Frost. Lawrence, Kansas, Allen Press and the
Association of Systematics Collections, 1985

The Audubon Society Field Guide to North American Reptiles and Amphibians by John L Behler
and F Wayne King. N.Y., Knopf, 1979

The Country Life *Book of the British Isles* ed. by Pat Morris. London, Country Life Books, 1979

A Field Guide to Australian Frogs by John Barker, Gordon C Grigg, and Michael J Tyler.
Sydney, Surrey, Beatty & Sons, 1995

Frogs by David Badger. Stillwater, MN, Voyageur Press, 1995

Frogs of the Northern Territory by Michael J Tyler and Margaret Davies. Darwin, Conservation
Commission of the Northern Territory, 1986

Reptiles & Amphibians of Australia by Harold G Cogger. Rev. ed. Sydney, Reed, 1983

Simon & Schuster's Guide to Reptiles and Amphibians of the World by Massimo Capula.
N.Y., Simon & Schuster, 1989

Internet Resources

Exploratorium: Frogs: http://www.exploratorium.edu/frogs/links.html
Excellent collection of links to other frog sites

Hamline University Center for Global Environmental Education:
http://cgee.hamline.edu/frogs/
A comprehensive frog site for teachers and students.

Australian National Botanic Gardens: http://www.anbg.gov.au/anbg/frogs/index.html
Information on a number of Australian garden frogs with sounds.

The Somewhat Amusing World of Frogs:
http://www.csu.edu.au/faculty/commerce/account/frogs/frog.htm
Lots of interesting information about frogs including jokes.

Frogs for Kids: http://www.pca.state.mn.us/kids/frogsforkids.html
Information on frog sounds and habitat threats, from Minnesota's Pollution Control Agency.

Frog Decline Reversal Project: http://www.fdrproject.org/
Based in North Queensland this organisation maintains a frog hospital.

2003, First U.S.edition
Published by Charlesbridge
85 Main Street, Watertown, MA 02472
617-926-0329 / www.charlesbridge.com

First published by Margaret Hamilton Books in 2002.
This edition is published under license from Margaret Hamilton Books,
a division of Scholastic Australia Pty. Limited.

Library of Congress Cataloging-in-Publication Data available upon request.

ISBN 1-57091-548-2 (reinforced for library use). ISBN 1-57091-549-0 (softcover)

Printed in Singapore by Tien Wah Press
(hc) 10 9 8 7 6 5 4 3 2 1
(sc) 10 9 8 7 6 5 4 3 2 1
The illustrations in this book were done in watercolors.
Typeset in Bernhard.